LOOK, LOOK AGAIN
SPORTS
PICTURE PUZZLES

by Matt Bruning

Capstone press

Mankato, Minnesota

HOW TO PLAY:

Look at the photo pair below. Now, look again! Can you spot the difference?

Do you see it? That's right! The hat color changed from red to blue.

Master the photo puzzles in this book in two easy steps:

1. Study the photo on the left.
2. Look at the photo on the right to spot the differences.

More Puzzle Fun:

• Challenge a friend to see who can solve the most puzzles.

• See how long it takes you and a friend to solve the same puzzle. Whoever solves the puzzle first wins!

TABLE OF CONTENTS

Let's start with an easy puzzle. Can you find
6 differences in this snowy photo?

Fore! You'll need to spot **6** differences to shoot par in this puzzle.

Start your engines! Spot **6** differences to race through this picture puzzle.

Let's make this puzzle a little harder. Find **8** changes while these players shoot hoops.

STREET THRASHER

See if you can find 8 differences
before the skater finishes his trick.

Can you spot 8 differences before these kite surfers blow away?

Wow! You're getting good at this. Let's see if you can find **10** differences here. Don't strike out!

Try to tackle the *10* differences
hidden in this football photo.

JUMPING JOCKEYS

Giddyap! Find **10** differences before you jump to the next puzzle.

**Think you're an expert? Not so fast.
Pick up the pace to find all 12 changes.**

Spot 12 differences before the next lap.

This is it! Prove you're a pro, and find
these last **12** differences.

ANSWER KEY

page 5

page 7

page 9

page 11

page 13

page 15

page 17

page 19

ANSWER KEY

page 21

page 23

page 25

page 27

Read More

Bruning, Matt. *Mighty Machines Picture Puzzles.* Look, Look Again. Mankato, Minn.: Capstone Press, 2010.

Marks, Jennifer L. *Fun and Games: A Spot-It Challenge.* Spot It. Mankato, Minn.: Capstone Press, 2009.

Internet Sites

FactHound offers a safe, fun way to find Internet sites related to this book. All of the sites on FactHound have been researched by our staff.

Here's all you do:

Visit *www.facthound.com*

FactHound will fetch the best sites for you!

A+ Books are published by Capstone Press,
151 Good Counsel Drive, P.O. Box 669, Mankato, Minnesota 56002.
www.capstonepress.com

 Books published by Capstone Press are manufactured with paper
containing at least 10 percent post-consumer waste.

Library of Congress Cataloging-in-Publication Data
Bruning, Matt.
    Sports picture puzzles / by Matt Bruning.
    p. cm. — (A+ books. Look, look again)
    Includes bibliographical references.
    Summary: "Simple text invites readers to spot the differences in sports-themed
picture puzzles" — Provided by publisher.
    ISBN 978-1-4296-3290-4 (library binding)
    ISBN 978-1-4296-3840-1 (pbk.)
    1. Picture puzzles — Juvenile literature. 2. Sports — Juvenile literature. I. Title. II. Series.
GV1507.P47B78 2010
793.73 — dc22   2009002763

Credits

Megan Peterson, editor; Matt Bruning, designer; Wanda Winch, media researcher

Photo Credits

CreativeMYK.com/Matt Gruber, cover (green leaf circle on T-shirt); Shutterstock/Herbert Kratky,
18, 19, 29 (bottom right); Shutterstock/Inc, 14, 15, 29 (top right); Shutterstock/Jeff R. Clow, cover
(skateboarder), 1, 12, 13, 29 (top left); Shutterstock/Jonathan Larsen, 22, 23, 26, 27, 30 (top right,
bottom right); Shutterstock/Junker, 2 (both), 6, 7, 28 (top right); Shutterstock/KPegg, 16, 17, 29
(bottom left); Shutterstock/Mayskyphoto, 10, 11, 28 (bottom right); Shutterstock/Morgan Lane
Photography, 5 (snowman); Shutterstock/Neil Roy Johnson, 20, 21, 30 (top left); Shutterstock/
Nicola Gavin, 8, 9, 28 (bottom left); Shutterstock/Nikolay Tonev, 24, 25, 30 (bottom left);
Shutterstock/Sportsphotographer.eu, 4, 5 (skier), 28 (top left); Shutterstock/Trinacria Photo, cover
(baseball bat and glove)

The publisher does not endorse products whose logos may appear on objects in images in this book.

Note to Parents, Teachers, and Librarians

Look, Look Again is an interactive set that supports literacy development and reading enjoyment.
Readers utilize visual discrimination skills to spot the differences in picture puzzles. Readers also
improve strategic and associative thinking skills by experimenting with different visual
search methods.